MEL BAY PRESENTS

101 BLUES PATTERNS FOR BASS GUITAR

BY LARRY MCCABE

CD CONTENTS

---

1 2 3 4 5 6 7 8 9 0

CONTENTS

INTRODUCTION

The blues bassist commands an enviable position. Possessing the ability to play patterns in a band almost from the start, (s)he has chosen a style that offers unlimited potential for artistic growth. And the added bonus is this: it is *fun* to play the blues on the bass guitar!

This collection showcases a wide variety of bass patterns that can be readily applied to blues recordings and performances, even by the novice. Many of the patterns have been time-tested and are mandatory in the repertoire of any serious bassist.

Included among the 101 patterns are ten standard blues turnarounds and ten standard blues endings that can be used in literally thousands of songs. In addition, the book provides several pages of valuable music theory and other information on blues progressions. Another feature is the companion compact disc, which is very helpful for students who are learning to read and count time.

It is my hope that this book will provide stimulation for students, organization for teachers, and reference for experienced players. Enjoy!

Larry McCabe
Tallahassee, Florida

HOW TO USE THIS BOOK

The blues bass patterns in this collection may be played on both the electric and the acoustic bass. Most of the patterns are not difficult to play, and the student may learn the examples in any order. One of the key features of this book is the potential for applying these patterns to recorded songs. There are thousands of rock and blues songs that the patterns can be applied to almost immediately, and the student is encouraged to learn to play along with recordings as soon as possible (see pg. 38 for a list of mail-order companies that sell blues records).

Some of the bass patterns in this book are played to a C7 chord; other patterns work with both C7 *and* Cmi7. In the blues, any pattern that fits the C7 chord will usually work with C9, C13, and the C major triad. Likewise, a Cmi7 pattern will usually sound fine with a Cmi9, Cmi13, and the C minor triad (C minor is written either Cmi or Cm).

For the sake of uniformity and ease of analysis, each bass pattern in this book uses the C note as its root tone. However, any pattern may be easily *transposed* to any other root tone; for example, move any C7 pattern up two frets to produce a D7 pattern.

New students are encouraged to study the introductory section which begins on the following page. Here, you will find vital information concerning blues progressions, transposition, timing, and pattern application. Finally, the list of creative projects on page 13 will help teachers organize lesson plans while encouraging students to develop a comprehensive approach to their studies.

THE TWELVE-BAR BLUES PROGRESSION

The *twelve-bar blues progression* is a standard song form which has been used for thousands of songs in every popular style. The following example illustrates a basic twelve-bar blues progression in the key of C major:

```
C7          C7          C7          C7
/ / / /     / / / /     / / / /     / / / /
F7          F7          C7          C7
/ / / /     / / / /     / / / /     / / / /
G7          F7          C7          C7
/ / / /     / / / /     / / / /     / / / /
```

The basic twelve-bar minor-key blues progression is played as follows (ex. in Cm):

```
Cm7         Cm7         Cm7         Cm7
/ / / /     / / / /     / / / /     / / / /
Fm7         Fm7         Cm7         Cm7
/ / / /     / / / /     / / / /     / / / /
Gm7         Fm7         Cm7         Cm7
/ / / /     / / / /     / / / /     / / / /
```

USING THE BASS PATTERNS TO PLAY ENTIRE SONGS

The following example shows how bass pattern #1 (pg. 15) can be transposed to the F7 and G7 chords to accompany a blues progression in C major:

Bass pattern #1 played through an entire blues progression

The use of one bass pattern (see above) for an entire blues progression is known as *ostinato* bass. This bass style was used extensively by boogie-woogie pianists such as Albert Ammons, Jimmy Yancey, Meade "Lux" Lewis, Pete Johnson, and Pinetop Smith. As a blues bassist, you will benefit greatly by listening to their records.

Patterns may be combined, of course. When you combine the patterns, you must listen carefully to be sure that they are organized in a way that makes good musical sense. Combining the patterns in new and different combinations is a great way for you to learn about creating your own bass lines.

VARIATIONS ON THE TWELVE-BAR PROGRESSION

There are many standard variations on the twelve-bar blues progression. Compare the following blues progressions with the twelve-bar blues progression in C major on page 6:

C7	F7	C7	C7
/ / / /	/ / / /	/ / / /	/ / / /
F7	F7	C7	C7
/ / / /	/ / / /	/ / / /	/ / / /
G7	F7	C7	G7
/ / / /	/ / / /	/ / / /	/ / / /

C7	F7	C7	C7
/ / / /	/ / / /	/ / / /	/ / / /
F7	F7	C7	C7
/ / / /	/ / / /	/ / / /	/ / / /
G7	F7	C7 F7	C7 G7
/ / / /	/ / / /	/ / / /	/ / / /

Many combinations of chords are possible for twelve-bar blues progressions (see page 37 for more examples). For further reference, see my Mel Bay book entitled *Blues Band Rhythm Guitar*, which contains a great variety of blues progressions, and teaches how to develop "jazzy" blues from the standard three-chord progressions.

THE EIGHT-BAR BLUES PROGRESSION

The *eight-bar blues progression* is a standard alternative to the twelve-bar blues progression. Here is a typical eight-bar blues in C:

```
C7          G7          F7          F7
/ / / /   / / / /   / / / /   / / / /
C7          G7          C7   F7   C7   G7
/ / / /   / / / /   / / / /   / / / /
```

After working with some of the twelve-bar progressions, try applying your patterns to the above progression. This will help you develop a feel for the eight-bar blues.

CHORD TONES

Besides keeping time, the bass player's main function is to *outline the accompanying chord.* This task is achieved by making frequent use of chord tones. Therefore, it is important for the bassist to be able to locate and play the notes in any given chord. Using the C major scale, we will now learn how to name the notes in four types of chords: major triads, minor triads, dominant seventh chords, and minor seventh chords.

The C major scale

1	2	3	4	5	6	7	8
C	D	E	F	G	A	B	C

The *major triad* contains the 1-3-5 tones of the scale; result: C = C, E, G.
The *minor triad* contains the 1-$\flat3$-5 tones of the scale; result: Cmi = C, E$\flat$, G.
The *dominant seventh chord* contains the 1-3-5-$\flat7$ tones of the scale; result: C7 = C, E, G, B$\flat$.
The *minor seventh chord* contains the 1-$\flat3$-5-$\flat7$ tones of the scale; result: Cmi7 = C, E$\flat$, G, B$\flat$.

The numerical group (1, 3, 5, etc.) comprising the chord tones is known as the *chord formula.* Always apply the chord formula to the major scale that corresponds to the chord you are naming; for example, the *G major triad* contains the 1-3-5 tones of the *G scale,* or G-B-D.

THE ROMAN NUMERAL CHORD SYSTEM

The *Roman numeral system* is a chord-numbering system that helps musicians understand how chords function. This system assigns a numerical identification to each chord, making it easy to transpose chord progressions from one key to another.

We will learn the Roman numeral system by first identifying the *main chords* in the key of C: C, F, and G7. In the key of C, the C chord is known as I because its root tone is the first tone in the corresponding scale (the C major scale). Similarly, the F chord functions as IV because its root is the fourth note in the C scale. That leaves us with only the G7 chord to label. The identification for G7 will require two characters, one for the position of the chord root in the C scale (V), and one for the chord type (7); thus, the G7 chord is called the V7 chord in the key of C.

It is important to realize that the function of a given chord is determined by the key of the moment; for example, the C chord is I in the key of C, IV in the key of G, V in the key of F, ♭VII in the key of D, II in the key of B♭, and so on.

The tonality of the blues is rather unique. In the major-key blues, the three main chords are usually voiced as dominant chords; therefore, the main chords for a blues tune in C major would be C7 (I7), F7 (IV7), and G7 (V7). These dominant chords produce the dissonant, "bluesy" harmony which is a main characteristic of the style.

Applying Roman numerals to the basic twelve-bar progression in C major (pg. 6), we can now sketch a model blues progression that can be transposed to any major key:

I7	I7	I7	I7
/ / / /	/ / / /	/ / / /	/ / / /
IV7	IV7	I7	I7
/ / / /	/ / / /	/ / / /	/ / / /
V7	IV7	I7	I7
/ / / /	/ / / /	/ / / /	/ / / /

The following is a model for the basic minor-key blues progression on page 6:

im7	im7	im7	im7
/ / / /	/ / / /	/ / / /	/ / /

ivm7	ivm7	im7	im7
/ / / /	/ / / /	/ / / /	/ / / /

vm7	ivm7	im7	im7
/ / / /	/ / / /	/ / / /	/ / / /

4/4 TIME AND 12/8 TIME

4/4 TIME
Patterns played in 4/4 time are known as *straight-time* patterns. Straight-time patterns are most often associated with rock (or blues/rock), but we do find urban blues songs that are in straight time; one that quickly comes to mind is "Killing Floor" by Howlin' Wolf. Straight-time patterns are counted in the conventional manner that is used when the beat is divided into two parts:

ONE and TWO and THREE and FOUR and

12/8 TIME
12/8 time is the meter most closely associated with the urban blues. 12/8 time is counted out in four *eighth-note triplet* units per measure:

ONE and a TWO and a THREE and a FOUR and a

12/8 songs have a *triplet feel.* Often, tunes with a triplet feel are played with a *shuffle rhythm* which may consist of either of the following variations:

Shuffle rhythm # 1   **Shuffle rhythm # 2**

A good way to learn to distinguish between these different rhythms is to listen to the tape that is available for this book. Blues records are also very instructive; pay special attention to the beat the drummer plays on the hi-hat or ride cymbal.

Some of the 4/4 patterns in this book can also be played in 12/8, and vice versa. Experiment with the patterns, and try to decide which ones sound good with both rhythms.

CREATIVE PROJECTS FOR THE MUSIC STUDENT

The following list of projects will help students learn to apply the patterns in this book to popular blues recordings and live performance situations.

1. Using the Roman numeral system, transpose each blues progression on page 37 to several other keys.
2. Memorize the I7, IV7, and V7 chords in all major keys.
3. Memorize the imi7, ivmi7, and vmi7 chord names in several minor keys. (Notice that the minor chords use lowercase Roman numerals.) Also, keep it in mind that V7 is often used instead of vmi7 in the minor blues.
4. Starting with bass pattern #1 (pg. 15), label the notes that make up each pattern by scale degree. For example, pattern #1 would be labeled as follows:

1-1-1-1-1-3-4-♯4-5

   As you label the patterns in this manner, you will learn these concepts:
   a) Some patterns contain only chord tones. These are called *arpeggios.*
   b) The ♭3 and ♭7 tones are used extensively in the blues. These notes are often called "blue notes."
   c) The ♯4 note (also called ♭5) is sometimes used to connect 4 to 5.
   d) The 6th tone is often used along with 1, 3, 5, and ♭7 for dominant (C7, F7, etc.) chord arpeggios.
5. Memorize the chord tones, and play the arpeggios for: all major triads, minor triads, dominant seventh chords, and minor seventh chords.
6. The C natural minor scale is C-D-E♭-F-G-A♭-B♭-C. For the C minor 7 chord, we would call E♭ "flat three," A♭ "flat six," and B♭ "flat seven." As you analyze the patterns that fit the minor chords, you will note the avoidance of the natural third.
7. Using patterns from this book, try to create several original blues accompaniments. You can start with a pattern on I7, and simply transpose it to IV7 and V7. (Of course, a two-bar I7 pattern will not fit into one bar of IV7 or V7, but sometimes you can modify a pattern to make it sound right.) If it sounds awkward, look for a way to modify it so that it will fit. The idea is to experiment, learn to create, and play tastefully. Do not try to mix too many different patterns into a single progression, or the music will lose its focus. For starters, try writing your accompaniments to the **blues progressions for practice** on page 37.
8. Write some original four-beat and eight-beat bass patterns.
9. Transcribe some bass lines from blues recordings of your own choice.

FOUR-BEAT PATTERNS
IN 12/8 TIME

Stevie Ray Vaughan
Photo by Dave Ranney

Patterns 1 to 32 fit C7 in 12/8 time

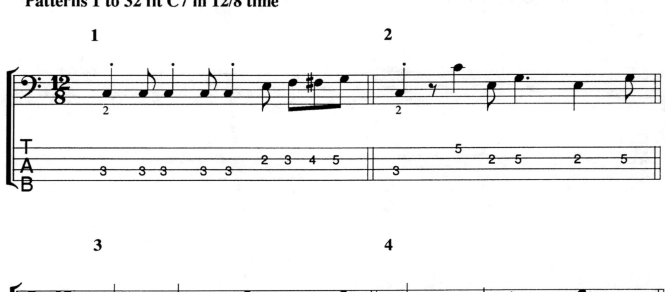

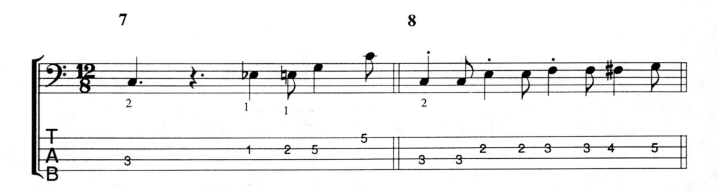

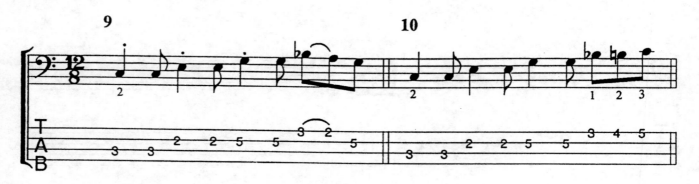

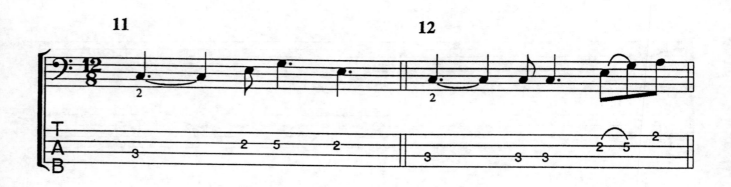

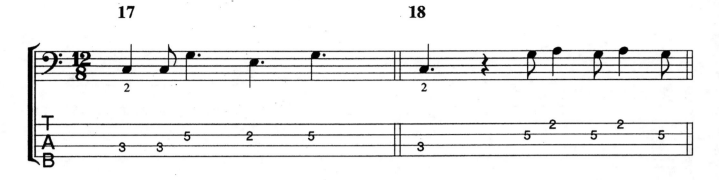

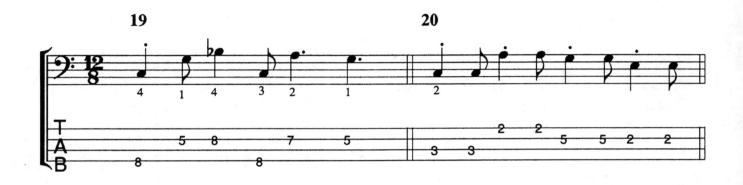

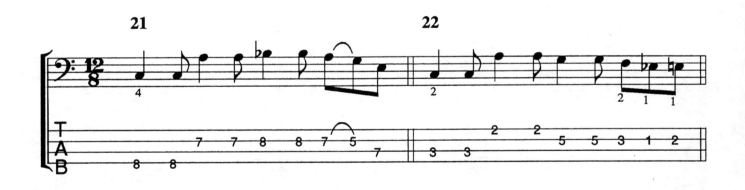

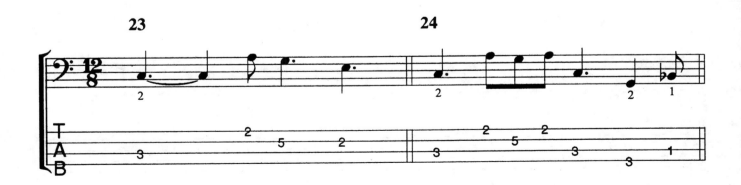

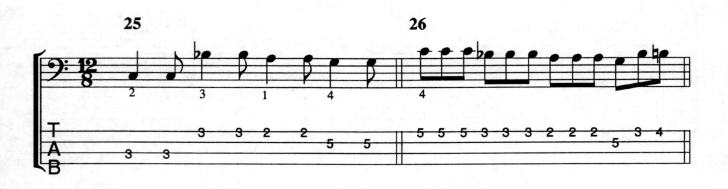

Patterns 33-52 fit C7 or Cmi7 in 12/8 time

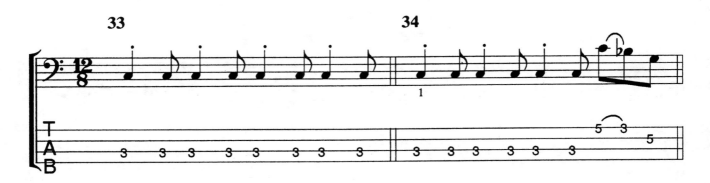

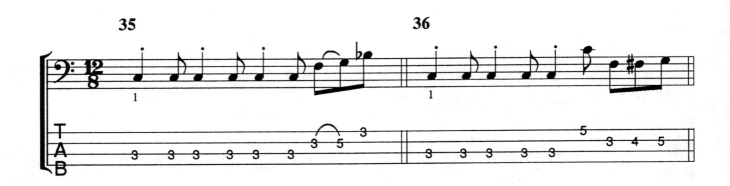

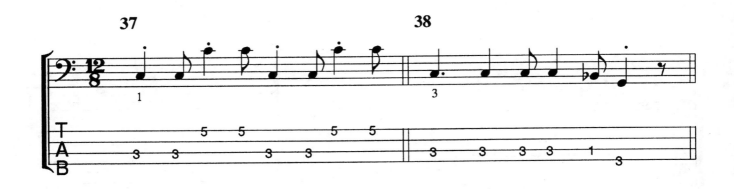

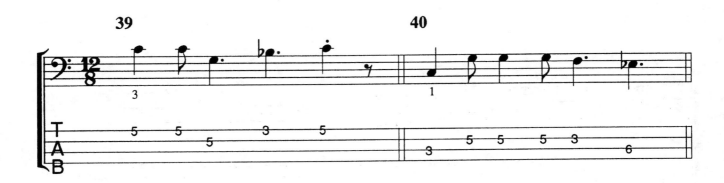

C7 or Cmi7 12/8 patterns, continued

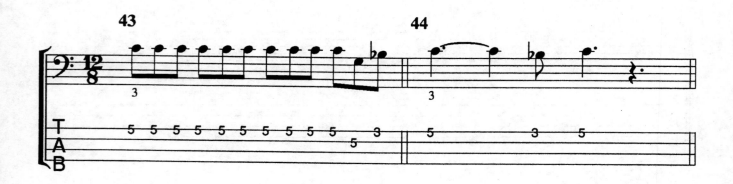

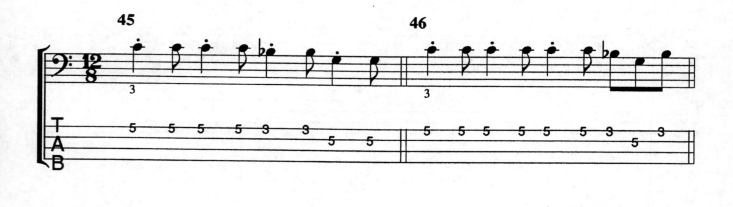

C7 or Cmi7 12/8 patterns, continued

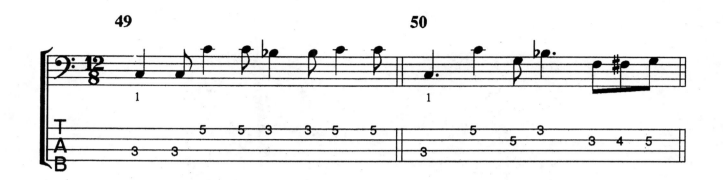

FOUR-BEAT PATTERNS
IN 4/4 TIME

Stevie Ray Vaughan
Photo by Dave Ranney

Patterns 53-60 fit C7 in 4/4 time

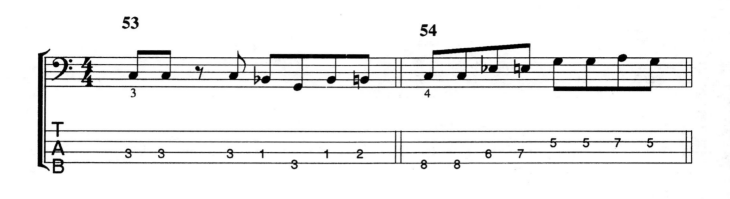

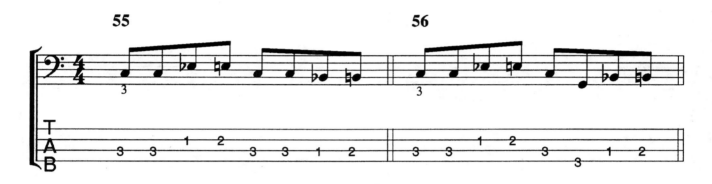

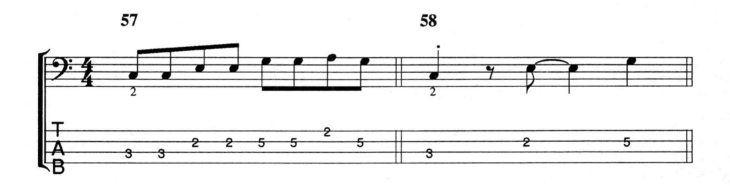

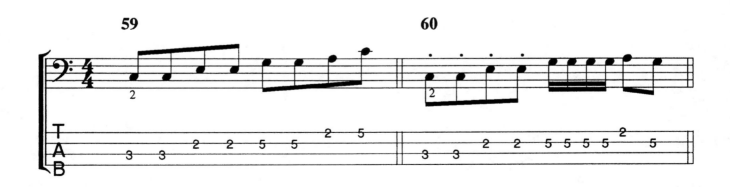

23

Patterns 61-65 fit C7 or Cmi7 in 4/4 time

EIGHT-BEAT PATTERNS
IN 12/8 TIME

Willie Dixon - 1983 S.F. Blues Festival
Photo by Stuart Brinin

Patterns 66-71 fit C7 in 12/8 time

66

67

68

69

C7 12/8 patterns, continued

70

71

Patterns 72-77 fit C7 or Cmi7 in 12/8 time

72

73

C7 or Cmi7 patterns, continued

74

75

76

77

EIGHT-BEAT PATTERNS
IN 4/4 TIME

Willie Dixon and Koko Taylor - Ann Arbor Blues Festival
Photo by Doug Fulton

Patterns 78-79 fit C7 in 4/4 time

78

79

Patterns 80-81 fit C7 or Cm7 in 4/4 time

80

81

TURNAROUNDS IN THE
KEY OF C

Magic Sam and Buffalo Bob - Ann Arbor Blues Festival
Photo by Doug Fulton

Patterns 82-91 are TURNAROUNDS in C

Optional chords are indicated by parentheses ( ).

Turnarounds in C, continued

*The first measure of ex. 90 could also be harmonized with F7 on beats 3 and 4.
 Another possibility would be A♭7 on the 3rd beat and G7 on the 4th beat.

ENDINGS IN THE
KEY OF C

Freddie King - The "Texas Cannonball"
Photo by Amy Van Singel

Patterns 92-101 are ENDINGS in C

BLUES PROGRESSIONS FOR PRACTICE

Students should use the following chord progressions as models for pattern application and practice. Transfer each progression to manuscript paper, and fill in a bass accompaniment. For best results, transpose each progression to several keys. Later, try to play your arrangements with blues recordings by Muddy Waters, Elmore James, Eric Clapton, and similar recording artists.

Blues progression #1

C7 (I7)   C7 (I7)   C7 (I7)   C7 (I7)
/ / / /   / / / /   / / / /   / / / /
F7 (IV7) F7 (IV7) C7 (I7)   C7 (I7)
/ / / /   / / / /   / / / /   / / / /
G7 (V7)   G7 (V7)   C7 (I7)   C7 (I7)
/ / / /   / / / /   / / / /   / / / /

Blues progression #2

C7 (I7)   C7 (I7)   C7 (I7)   C7 (I7)
/ / / /   / / / /   / / / /   / / / /
F7 (IV7) F7 (IV7) C7 (I7)   C7 (I7)
/ / / /   / / / /   / / / /   / / / /
G7 (V7)   F7 (IV7) C7 (I7)   C7 (I7)
/ / / /   / / / /   / / / /   / / / /

Blues progression #3

C7 (I7)   F7 (IV7) C7 (I7)   C7 (I7)
/ / / /   / / / /   / / / /   / / / /
F7 (IV7) F7 (IV7) C7 (I7)   C7 (I7)
/ / / /   / / / /   / / / /   / / / /
G7 (V7)   F7 (IV7) C7 (I7)   C7 (I7)
/ / / /   / / / /   / / / /   / / / /

Blues progression #4

C7 (I7)   C7 (I7)   C7 (I7)   C7 (I7)
/ / / /   / / / /   / / / /   / / / /
F7 (IV7) F7 (IV7) C7 (I7)   C7 (I7)
/ / / /   / / / /   / / / /   / / / /
G7 (V7)   F7 (IV7) C7 (I7)   G7 (V7)
/ / / /   / / / /   / / / /   / / / /

Blues progression #5

Cm7 (im7) Cm7 (im7) Cm7 (im7) Cm7 (im7)
/ / / /   / / / /   / / / /   / / / /
Fm7 (ivm7) Fm7 (ivm7) Cm7 (im7) Cm7 (im7)
/ / / /   / / / /   / / / /   / / / /
G7 (V7)   Fm7 (ivm7) Cm7 (im7) G7 (V7)
/ / / /   / / / /   / / / /   / / / /

Blues progression #6

Cm7 (im7) Fm7 (ivm7) Cm7 (im7) Cm7 (im7)
/ / / /   / / / /   / / / /   / / / /
Fm7 (ivm7) Fm7 (ivm7) Cm7 (im7) Cm7 (im7)
/ / / /   / / / /   / / / /   / / / /
G7 (V7) A♭7 (♭VI7)G7 (V7) Cm7 (im7) G7 (V7)
/ / / / / /   / /   / / / / / / / /

Blues progression #7

C7 (I7) G7 (V7) F7 (IV7) F7 (IV7) C7 (I7) G7 (V7) C7 (I7) F7 (IV7) C7 (I7) G7 (V7)
/ / / /   / / / /   / / / /   / / / /   / / / /   / / / /   / / / /   / / / /   / / / /   / / / /

SOURCES FOR BLUES RECORDINGS

Perhaps you live in a town where you are able to purchase blues albums from your local record shop. If not, each of the following mail-order suppliers and record companies carries a fine selection of blues albums.

CADENCE MAGAZINE
Cadence Building
Redwood, NY 13679

DELMARK RECORDS
4121 N. Rockwell
Chicago, IL 60618

ELDERLY INSTRUMENTS
1100 N. Washington
PO Box 14210
Lansing, MI 48901

ROOSTER BLUES RECORDS
Stackhouse/Delta Record Mart
232 Sunflower Avenue
Clarksdale, MS 38614

ROOTS 'N RHYTHM
6921 Stockton Ave.
El Cerrito, CA 94530

ROUNDUP RECORDS
1 Camp Street
Cambridge, MA 02140

OTHER MEL BAY BOOKS BY LARRY McCABE

**Anthology of American Rock and Roll Bass Styles
(book/CD set)**

**Anthology of American Rock and Roll Guitar Styles
(book/CD set)**

Blues Band Rhythm Guitar

Blues, Boogie, and Rock Guitar

Country Lead Guitar

101 Blues Turnaround Licks for Guitar

101 Nashville Style Country Guitar Licks

You Can Teach Yourself ® Song Writing